Tyler and Riley

By Selena Millman

Tyler and Riley
By Selena Millman

ISBN: 978-0-359-75077-1

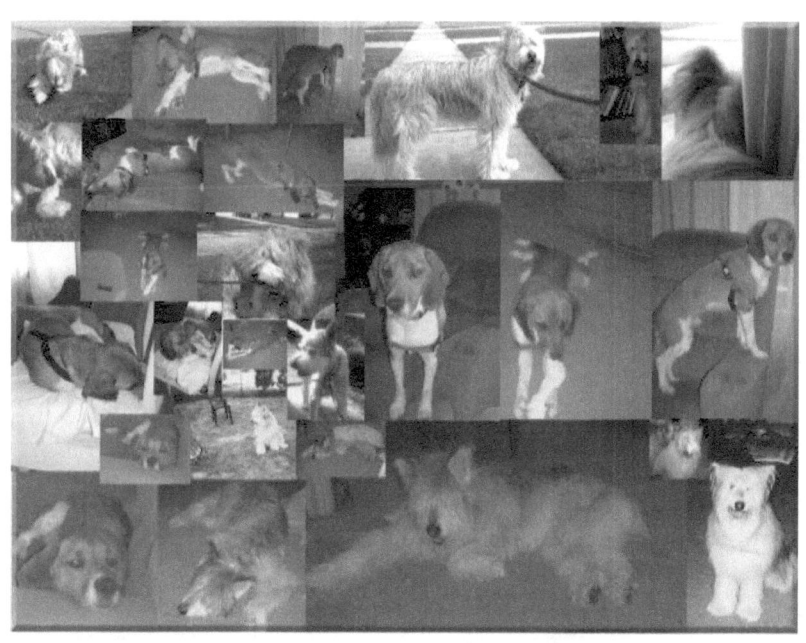

My name is Tyler.

They are not sure what breed I am but my family doesn't care.

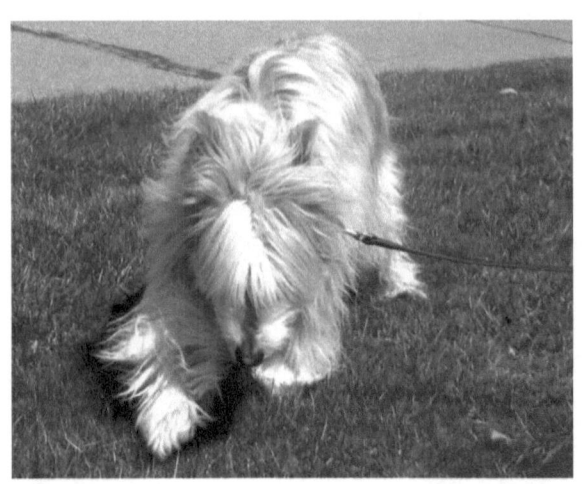

My name is Riley.

I'm a Beagle mix.

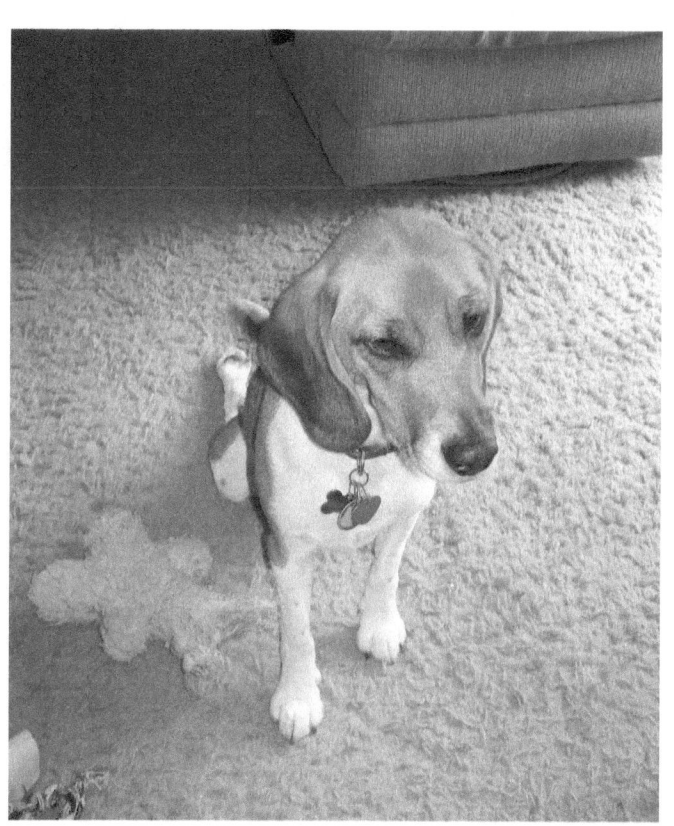

I was adopted when I was a puppy.

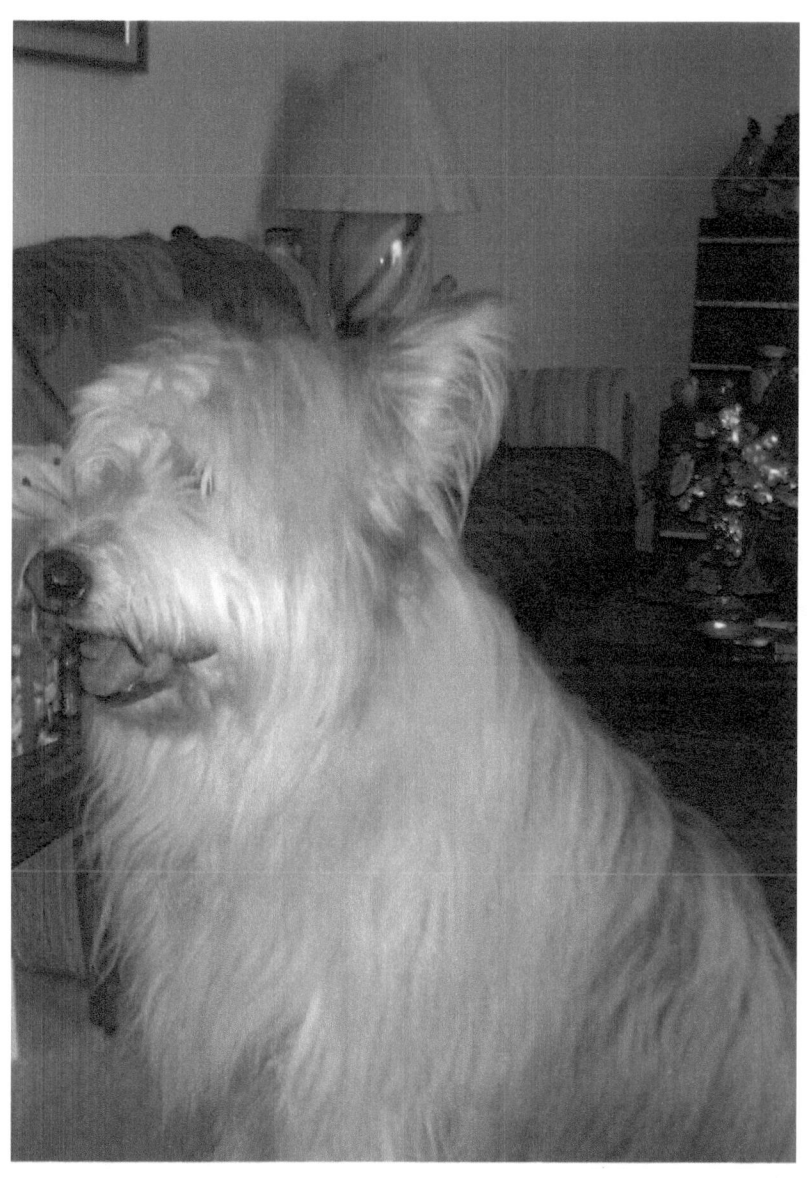

I was adopted when I was 3.

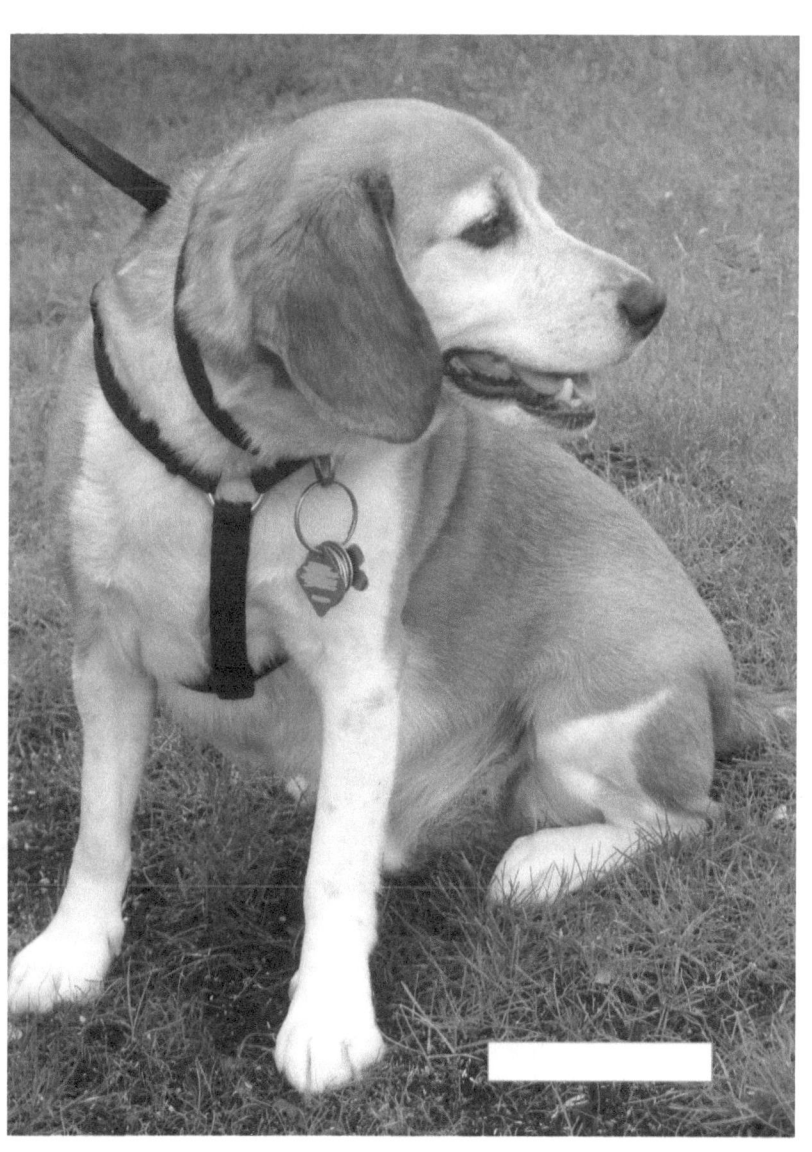

I started whining and they took me home.

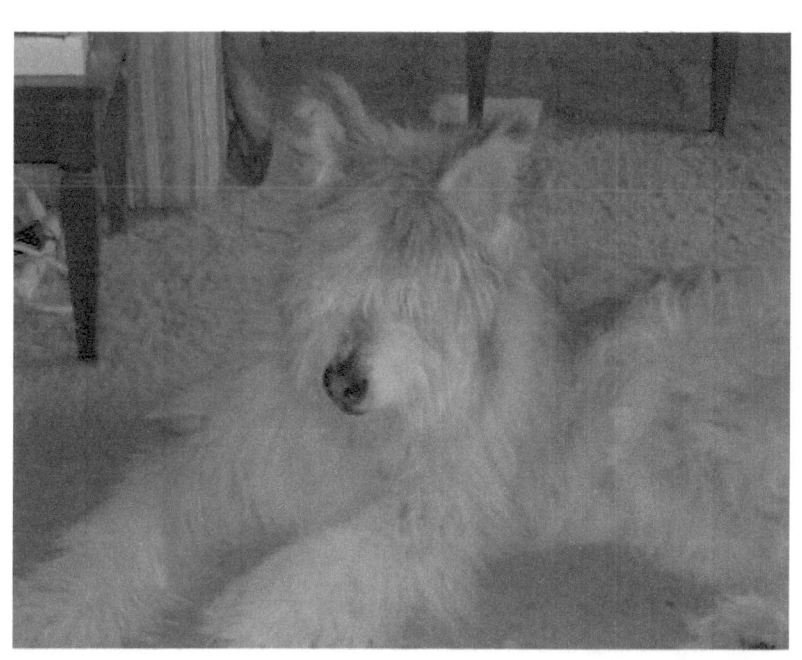

They just choose me.

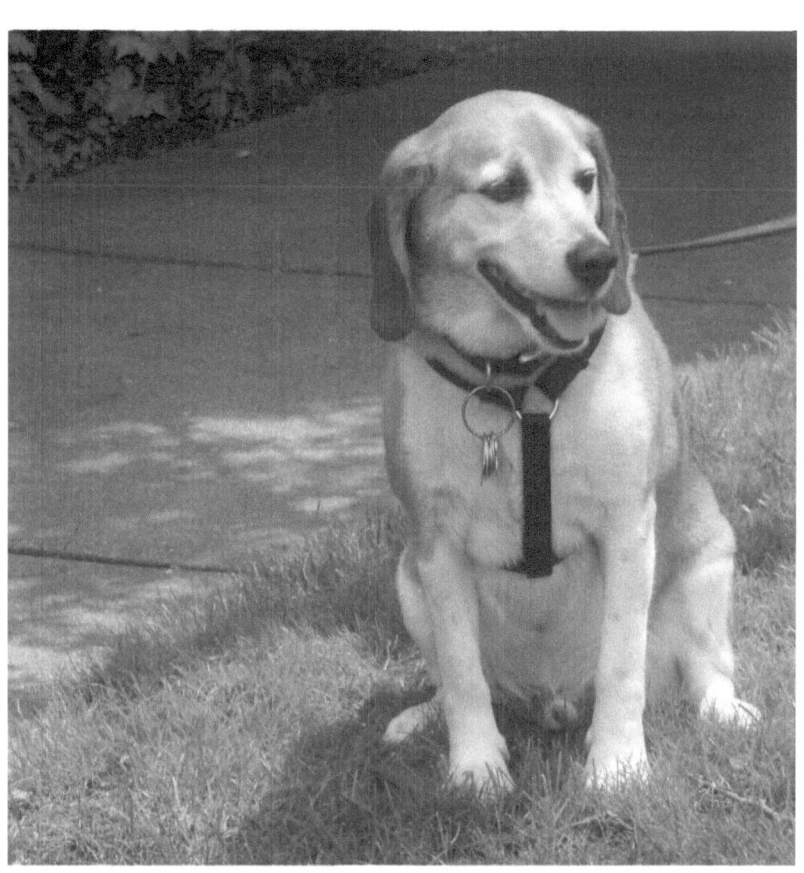

I'm usually pretty calm.

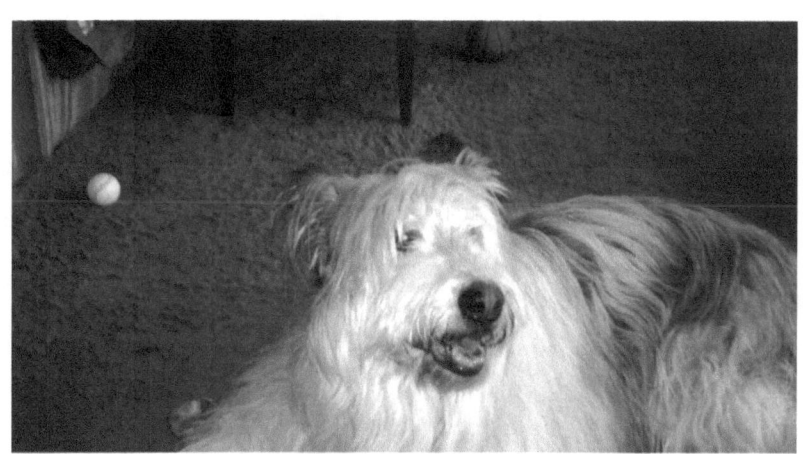

I'm usually hyper.

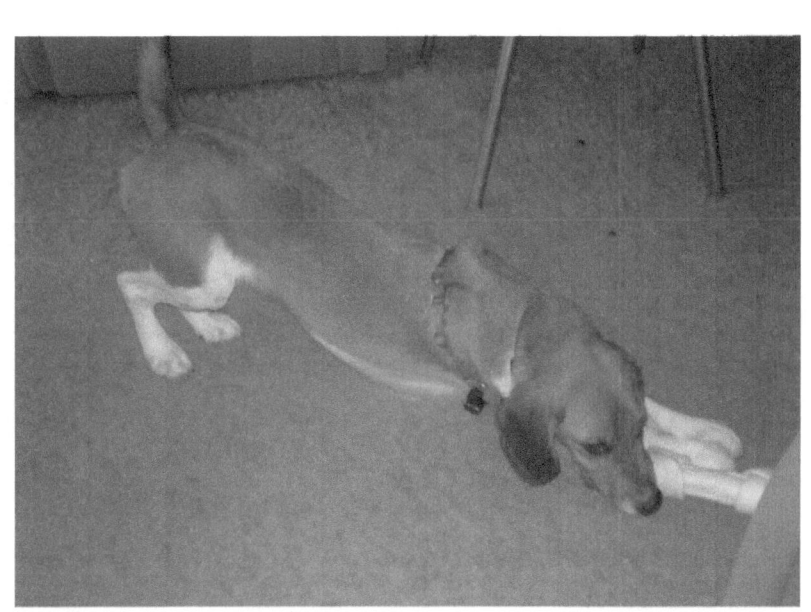

I like to give sneak kisses.

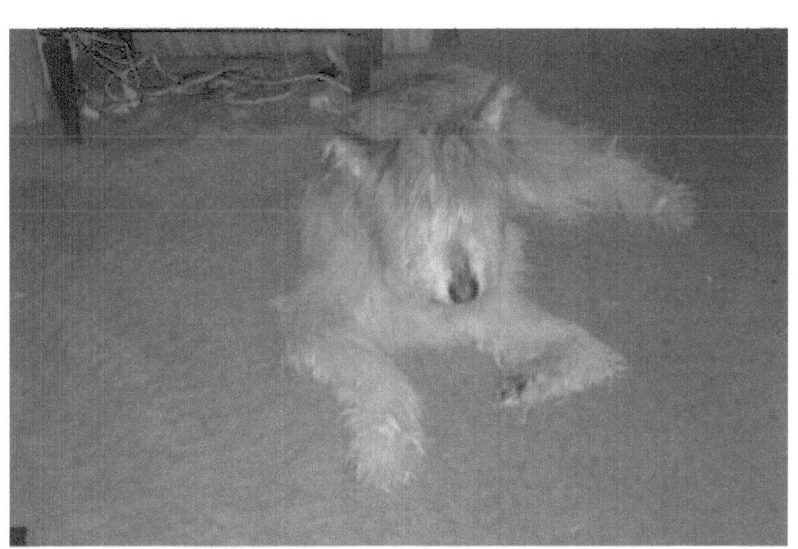

I get in your face and kiss you.

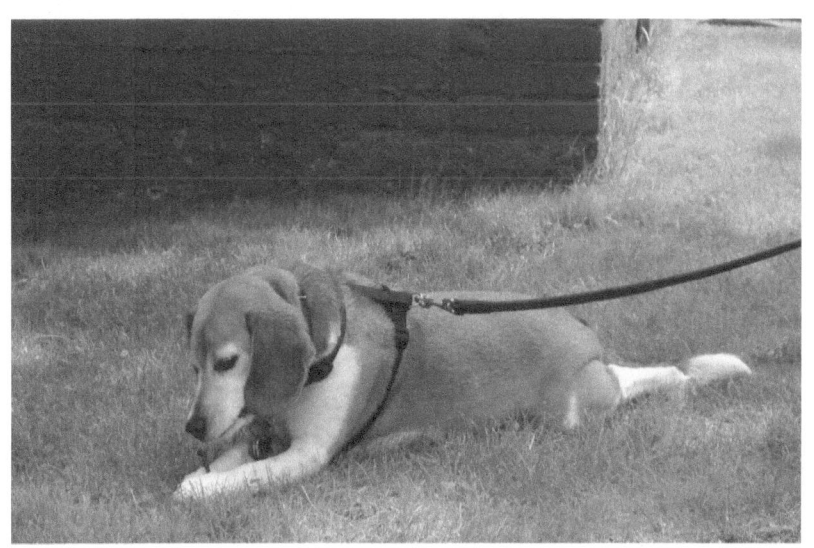

I just want to love you and for you to love me.

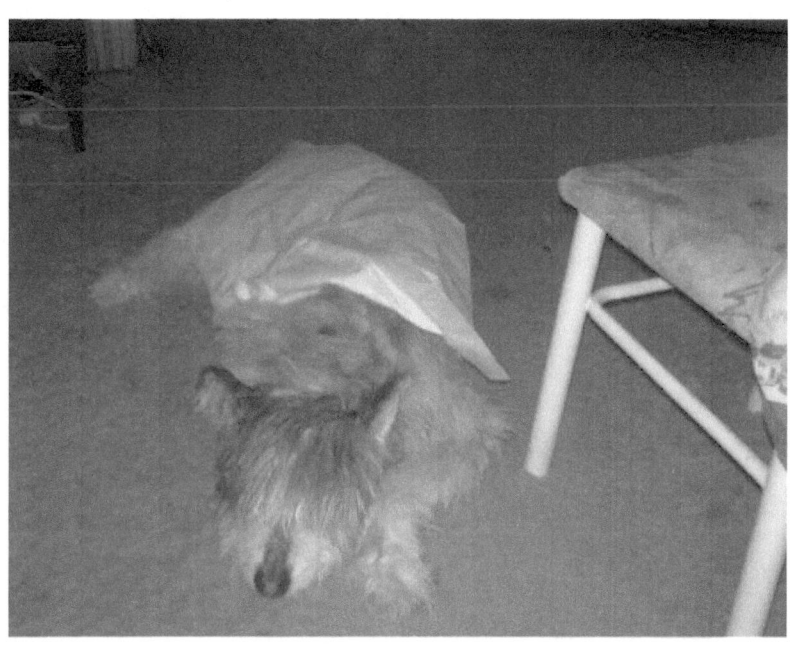

I also just want to love you and for you to love me.

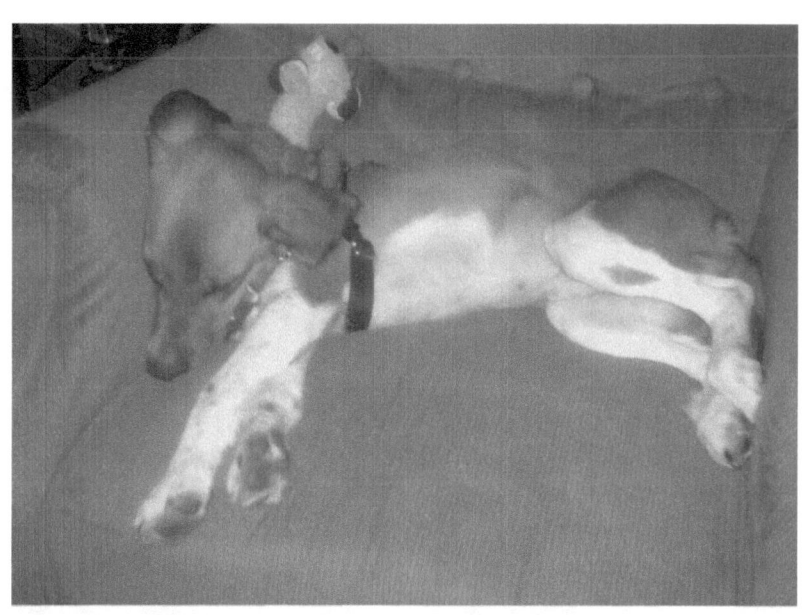

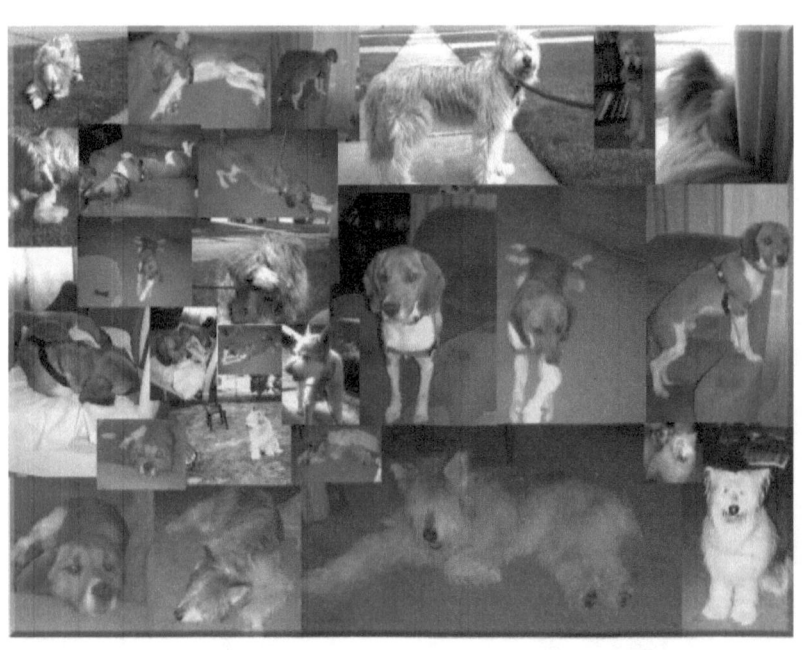

Tyler and Riley

All Photos

http://www.lulu.com/spotlight/heal4michael

httpwww.lulu.comshopselena-millmantyler-and-
rileypaperbackproduct-24150618.html

Tyler and Riley are dogs that my family adopted. They were both great dogs. I love and miss them.

I wish I had more photos of them both. It was years later that I really got into photography and got a great camera.

Selena Millman

June 24, 2019

Buy my Books and Photos at
http://www.lulu.com/heal4michael

Search Selena Millman at
http://www.amazon.com

Selena's Books & Devotions:
http://selenasbooksanddevotions.webs.com/

My Devotional Pages:
(Sermon Notes, Scripture, and Devotions)
http://heart4jesus.webs.com/
http://loveforjesus.webs.com/

My Books:
http://booksbyselena.webs.com/

Creative Page:
http://all4ty.webs.com/

www.ingramcontent.com/pod-product-compliance
Lightning Source LLC
Chambersburg PA
CBHW020959180526
45163CB00006B/2430